Personal Recipe Book

Personal Recipe Book
An M&M Publications Creation.
Printed by Createspace, an Amazon.com
Company.

ISBN-13: 978-1523237012
ISBN-10: 1523237015

Owner:

_____

_____

_____

RECIPES

Recipe name: _____

Ingredients: _____

_____   _____

_____   _____

_____   _____

_____   _____

_____

Cooking Time: _____

Portions: _____

Preparation Process: _____

_____

_____

_____

_____

_____

_____

_____

_____

_____

_____

_____

_____

_____

_____

_____

_____

_____

Recipe name: _____

Ingredients: _____

_____   _____

_____   _____

_____   _____

_____   _____

_____   _____

Cooking Time: _____

Portions: _____

Preparation Process: _____

_____

_____

_____

_____

_____

_____

_____

_____

_____

_____

_____

_____

_____

_____

_____

_____

_____

_____

_____

_____

Recipe name: _____
Ingredients: _____

_____ _____

_____ _____

_____ _____

_____ _____

_____ _____

Cooking Time: _____
Portions: _____
Preparation Process: _____

_____

_____

_____

_____

_____

_____

_____

_____

_____

_____

_____

_____

_____

_____

_____

_____

_____

_____

Recipe name: _____

Ingredients: _____

_____ _____

_____ _____

_____ _____

_____ _____

_____ _____

Cooking Time: _____

Portions: _____

Preparation Process: _____

_____

_____

_____

_____

_____

_____

_____

_____

_____

_____

_____

_____

_____

_____

_____

_____

_____

Recipe name: _____

Ingredients: _____

_____ _____

_____ _____

_____ _____

_____ _____

_____ _____

Cooking Time: _____

Portions: _____

Preparation Process: _____

_____

_____

_____

_____

_____

_____

_____

_____

_____

_____

_____

_____

_____

_____

_____

_____

_____

Recipe name: _____

Ingredients: _____

_____   _____

_____   _____

_____   _____

_____   _____

_____   _____

Cooking Time: _____

Portions: _____

Preparation Process: _____

_____

_____

_____

_____

_____

_____

_____

_____

_____

_____

_____

_____

_____

_____

_____

_____

_____

_____

Recipe name: _____
Ingredients: _____

_____ _____

_____ _____

_____ _____

_____ _____

_____ _____

Cooking Time: _____
Portions: _____
Preparation Process: _____

_____

_____

_____

_____

_____

_____

_____

_____

_____

_____

_____

_____

_____

_____

_____

_____

_____

Recipe name: _____

Ingredients: _____

_____   _____

_____   _____

_____   _____

_____   _____

_____   _____

Cooking Time: _____

Portions: _____

Preparation Process: _____

_____

_____

_____

_____

_____

_____

_____

_____

_____

_____

_____

_____

_____

_____

_____

_____

_____

_____

Recipe name: _____

Ingredients: _____

_____ _____

_____ _____

_____ _____

_____ _____

_____ _____

Cooking Time: _____

Portions: _____

Preparation Process:_____

_____

_____

_____

_____

_____

_____

_____

_____

_____

_____

_____

_____

_____

_____

_____

_____

_____

_____

Recipe name: _____

Ingredients: _____

_____ _____

_____ _____

_____ _____

_____ _____

_____ _____

Cooking Time: _____

Portions: _____

Preparation Process: _____

_____

_____

_____

_____

_____

_____

_____

_____

_____

_____

_____

_____

_____

_____

_____

_____

_____

_____

Recipe name: _____

Ingredients: _____

_____ _____

_____ _____

_____ _____

_____ _____

_____ _____

Cooking Time: _____

Portions: _____

Preparation Process: _____

_____

_____

_____

_____

_____

_____

_____

_____

_____

_____

_____

_____

_____

_____

_____

_____

_____

_____

_____

_____

_____

Recipe name: _____

Ingredients: _____

_____   _____

_____   _____

_____   _____

_____   _____

_____   _____

Cooking Time: _____

Portions: _____

Preparation Process: _____

_____

_____

_____

_____

_____

_____

_____

_____

_____

_____

_____

_____

_____

_____

_____

_____

_____

_____

Recipe name: _____

Ingredients: _____

_____ _____

_____ _____

_____ _____

_____ _____

_____ _____

Cooking Time: _____

Portions: _____

Preparation Process: _____

_____

_____

_____

_____

_____

_____

_____

_____

_____

_____

_____

_____

_____

_____

_____

_____

_____

_____

Recipe name: _____

Ingredients: _____

_____   _____

_____   _____

_____   _____

_____   _____

_____   _____

Cooking Time: _____

Portions: _____

Preparation Process:_____

_____

_____

_____

_____

_____

_____

_____

_____

_____

_____

_____

_____

_____

_____

_____

_____

_____

Recipe name: _____
Ingredients: _____

_____   _____
_____   _____
_____   _____
_____   _____
_____   _____

Cooking Time: _____
Portions: _____
Preparation Process:_____

_____
_____
_____
_____
_____
_____
_____
_____
_____
_____
_____
_____
_____
_____
_____
_____
_____
_____

Recipe name: _____

Ingredients: _____

_____   _____

_____   _____

_____   _____

_____   _____

_____   _____

Cooking Time: _____

Portions: _____

Preparation Process: _____

_____

_____

_____

_____

_____

_____

_____

_____

_____

_____

_____

_____

_____

_____

_____

_____

_____

_____

Recipe name: _____

Ingredients: _____

_____   _____

_____   _____

_____   _____

_____   _____

_____   _____

Cooking Time: _____

Portions: _____

Preparation Process: _____

_____

_____

_____

_____

_____

_____

_____

_____

_____

_____

_____

_____

_____

_____

_____

_____

_____

_____

Recipe name: _____

Ingredients: _____

_____   _____

_____   _____

_____   _____

_____   _____

_____   _____

Cooking Time: _____

Portions: _____

Preparation Process:_____

_____

_____

_____

_____

_____

_____

_____

_____

_____

_____

_____

_____

_____

_____

_____

_____

Recipe name: _____

Ingredients: _____

_____ _____

_____ _____

_____ _____

_____ _____

_____ _____

Cooking Time: _____

Portions: _____

Preparation Process: _____

_____

_____

_____

_____

_____

_____

_____

_____

_____

_____

_____

_____

_____

_____

_____

_____

_____

_____

Recipe name: _____

Ingredients: _____

_____ _____

_____ _____

_____ _____

_____ _____

_____ _____

Cooking Time: _____

Portions: _____

Preparation Process: _____

_____

_____

_____

_____

_____

_____

_____

_____

_____

_____

_____

_____

_____

_____

_____

_____

_____

_____

Recipe name: _____

Ingredients: _____

_____   _____

_____   _____

_____   _____

_____   _____

_____   _____

Cooking Time: _____

Portions: _____

Preparation Process: _____

_____

_____

_____

_____

_____

_____

_____

_____

_____

_____

_____

_____

_____

_____

_____

_____

_____

Recipe name: _____

Ingredients: _____

_____   _____

_____   _____

_____   _____

_____   _____

_____   _____

Cooking Time: _____

Portions: _____

Preparation Process: _____

_____

_____

_____

_____

_____

_____

_____

_____

_____

_____

_____

_____

_____

_____

_____

_____

_____

_____

Recipe name: _____

Ingredients: _____

_____ _____

_____ _____

_____ _____

_____ _____

_____ _____

Cooking Time: _____

Portions: _____

Preparation Process: _____

_____

_____

_____

_____

_____

_____

_____

_____

_____

_____

_____

_____

_____

_____

_____

_____

_____

_____

_____

_____

_____

Recipe name: _____

Ingredients: _____

_____ _____

_____ _____

_____ _____

_____ _____

_____ _____

Cooking Time: _____

Portions: _____

Preparation Process: _____

_____

_____

_____

_____

_____

_____

_____

_____

_____

_____

_____

_____

_____

_____

_____

_____

_____

Recipe name: _____

Ingredients: _____

_____ _____

_____ _____

_____ _____

_____ _____

_____ _____

Cooking Time: _____

Portions: _____

Preparation Process:_____

_____

_____

_____

_____

_____

_____

_____

_____

_____

_____

_____

_____

_____

_____

_____

_____

_____

Recipe name: _____

Ingredients: _____

_____   _____

_____   _____

_____   _____

_____   _____

_____   _____

Cooking Time: _____

Portions: _____

Preparation Process: _____

_____

_____

_____

_____

_____

_____

_____

_____

_____

_____

_____

_____

_____

_____

_____

_____

_____

_____

Recipe name: _____
Ingredients: _____

_____ _____

_____ _____

_____ _____

_____ _____

_____ _____

Cooking Time: _____
Portions: _____
Preparation Process: _____

_____

_____

_____

_____

_____

_____

_____

_____

_____

_____

_____

_____

_____

_____

_____

_____

_____

_____

Recipe name: _____

Ingredients: _____

_____ _____

_____ _____

_____ _____

_____ _____

_____ _____

Cooking Time: _____

Portions: _____

Preparation Process: _____

_____

_____

_____

_____

_____

_____

_____

_____

_____

_____

_____

_____

_____

_____

_____

_____

_____

_____

_____

Recipe name: _____
Ingredients: _____

_____   _____
_____   _____
_____   _____
_____   _____
_____   _____

Cooking Time: _____
Portions: _____
Preparation Process: _____

_____
_____
_____
_____
_____
_____
_____
_____
_____
_____
_____
_____
_____
_____
_____
_____
_____
_____
_____
_____
_____

Recipe name: _____

Ingredients: _____

_____   _____

_____   _____

_____   _____

_____   _____

_____   _____

Cooking Time: _____

Portions: _____

Preparation Process: _____

_____

_____

_____

_____

_____

_____

_____

_____

_____

_____

_____

_____

_____

_____

_____

_____

_____

Recipe name: _____

Ingredients: _____

_____   _____

_____   _____

_____   _____

_____   _____

_____   _____

Cooking Time: _____

Portions: _____

Preparation Process: _____

_____

_____

_____

_____

_____

_____

_____

_____

_____

_____

_____

_____

_____

_____

_____

_____

_____

Recipe name: _____

Ingredients: _____

_____   _____

_____   _____

_____   _____

_____   _____

_____   _____

Cooking Time: _____

Portions: _____

Preparation Process: _____

_____

_____

_____

_____

_____

_____

_____

_____

_____

_____

_____

_____

_____

_____

_____

_____

_____

_____

_____

Recipe name: _____

Ingredients: _____

_____ _____

_____ _____

_____ _____

_____ _____

_____ _____

Cooking Time: _____

Portions: _____

Preparation Process: _____

_____

_____

_____

_____

_____

_____

_____

_____

_____

_____

_____

_____

_____

_____

_____

_____

_____

Recipe name: _____

Ingredients: _____

_____   _____

_____   _____

_____   _____

_____   _____

_____   _____

Cooking Time: _____

Portions: _____

Preparation Process: _____

_____

_____

_____

_____

_____

_____

_____

_____

_____

_____

_____

_____

_____

_____

_____

_____

_____

_____

_____

Recipe name: _____

Ingredients: _____

_____   _____

_____   _____

_____   _____

_____   _____

_____   _____

Cooking Time: _____

Portions: _____

Preparation Process: _____

_____

_____

_____

_____

_____

_____

_____

_____

_____

_____

_____

_____

_____

_____

_____

_____

_____

_____

_____

Recipe name: _____
Ingredients: _____

_____   _____
_____   _____
_____   _____
_____   _____
_____   _____

Cooking Time: _____
Portions: _____
Preparation Process: _____

_____
_____
_____
_____
_____
_____
_____
_____
_____
_____
_____
_____
_____
_____
_____
_____
_____
_____

Recipe name: _____

Ingredients: _____

_____   _____

_____   _____

_____   _____

_____   _____

_____

Cooking Time: _____

Portions: _____

Preparation Process: _____

_____

_____

_____

_____

_____

_____

_____

_____

_____

_____

_____

_____

_____

_____

_____

_____

_____

_____

Recipe name: _____

Ingredients: _____

_____ _____

_____ _____

_____ _____

_____ _____

_____ _____

Cooking Time: _____

Portions: _____

Preparation Process: _____

_____

_____

_____

_____

_____

_____

_____

_____

_____

_____

_____

_____

_____

_____

_____

_____

_____

_____

_____

Recipe name: _____
Ingredients: _____

_____   _____
_____   _____
_____   _____
_____   _____
_____   _____

Cooking Time: _____
Portions: _____
Preparation Process:_____

_____
_____
_____
_____
_____
_____
_____
_____
_____
_____
_____
_____
_____
_____
_____
_____
_____
_____

Recipe name: _____

Ingredients: _____

_____   _____

_____   _____

_____   _____

_____   _____

_____   _____

Cooking Time: _____

Portions: _____

Preparation Process: _____

_____

_____

_____

_____

_____

_____

_____

_____

_____

_____

_____

_____

_____

_____

_____

_____

_____

Recipe name: _____

Ingredients: _____

_____ _____

_____ _____

_____ _____

_____ _____

_____ _____

Cooking Time: _____

Portions: _____

Preparation Process: _____

_____

_____

_____

_____

_____

_____

_____

_____

_____

_____

_____

_____

_____

_____

_____

_____

_____

_____

_____

Recipe name: _____

Ingredients: _____

_____   _____

_____   _____

_____   _____

_____   _____

_____   _____

Cooking Time: _____

Portions: _____

Preparation Process:_____

_____

_____

_____

_____

_____

_____

_____

_____

_____

_____

_____

_____

_____

_____

_____

_____

_____

Recipe name: _____

Ingredients: _____

_____ _____

_____ _____

_____ _____

_____ _____

_____ _____

Cooking Time: _____

Portions: _____

Preparation Process: _____

_____

_____

_____

_____

_____

_____

_____

_____

_____

_____

_____

_____

_____

_____

_____

_____

_____

Recipe name: _____

Ingredients: _____

_____   _____

_____   _____

_____   _____

_____   _____

_____   _____

Cooking Time: _____

Portions: _____

Preparation Process: _____

_____

_____

_____

_____

_____

_____

_____

_____

_____

_____

_____

_____

_____

_____

_____

_____

_____

_____

Recipe name: _____
Ingredients: _____

_____   _____
_____   _____
_____   _____
_____   _____
_____   _____

Cooking Time: _____
Portions: _____
Preparation Process:_____

_____
_____
_____
_____
_____
_____
_____
_____
_____
_____
_____
_____
_____
_____
_____
_____
_____
_____

Recipe name: _____

Ingredients: _____

_____   _____

_____   _____

_____   _____

_____   _____

_____   _____

Cooking Time: _____

Portions: _____

Preparation Process: _____

_____

_____

_____

_____

_____

_____

_____

_____

_____

_____

_____

_____

_____

_____

_____

_____

_____

_____

Recipe name: _____

Ingredients: _____

_____   _____

_____   _____

_____   _____

_____   _____

_____   _____

Cooking Time: _____

Portions: _____

Preparation Process: _____

_____

_____

_____

_____

_____

_____

_____

_____

_____

_____

_____

_____

_____

_____

_____

_____

_____

_____

_____

Recipe name: _____
Ingredients: _____

_____   _____
_____   _____
_____   _____
_____   _____
_____   _____

Cooking Time: _____
Portions: _____
Preparation Process: _____

_____
_____
_____
_____
_____
_____
_____
_____
_____
_____
_____
_____
_____
_____
_____
_____
_____
_____

Recipe name: _____

Ingredients: _____

_____   _____

_____   _____

_____   _____

_____   _____

_____   _____

Cooking Time: _____

Portions: _____

Preparation Process:_____

_____

_____

_____

_____

_____

_____

_____

_____

_____

_____

_____

_____

_____

_____

_____

_____

_____

_____

Recipe name: _____

Ingredients: _____

_____ _____

_____ _____

_____ _____

_____ _____

_____ _____

Cooking Time: _____

Portions: _____

Preparation Process: _____

_____

_____

_____

_____

_____

_____

_____

_____

_____

_____

_____

_____

_____

_____

_____

_____

_____

_____

_____

Recipe name: _____

Ingredients: _____

_____ _____

_____ _____

_____ _____

_____ _____

_____ _____

Cooking Time: _____

Portions: _____

Preparation Process: _____

_____

_____

_____

_____

_____

_____

_____

_____

_____

_____

_____

_____

_____

_____

_____

_____

Recipe name: _____

Ingredients: _____

_____   _____

_____   _____

_____   _____

_____   _____

_____   _____

Cooking Time: _____

Portions: _____

Preparation Process: _____

_____

_____

_____

_____

_____

_____

_____

_____

_____

_____

_____

_____

_____

_____

_____

_____

_____

_____

_____

Recipe name: _____

Ingredients: _____

_____ _____

_____ _____

_____ _____

_____ _____

_____ _____

Cooking Time: _____

Portions: _____

Preparation Process:_____

_____

_____

_____

_____

_____

_____

_____

_____

_____

_____

_____

_____

_____

_____

_____

_____

_____

_____

_____

Recipe name: _____

Ingredients: _____

_____   _____

_____   _____

_____   _____

_____   _____

_____   _____

Cooking Time: _____

Portions: _____

Preparation Process: _____

_____

_____

_____

_____

_____

_____

_____

_____

_____

_____

_____

_____

_____

_____

_____

_____

_____

_____

_____

Recipe name: _____
Ingredients: _____

_____   _____
_____   _____
_____   _____
_____   _____
_____   _____

Cooking Time: _____
Portions: _____
Preparation Process: _____

_____
_____
_____
_____
_____
_____
_____
_____
_____
_____
_____
_____
_____
_____
_____
_____
_____
_____

Recipe name: _____

Ingredients: _____

_____   _____

_____   _____

_____   _____

_____   _____

_____   _____

Cooking Time: _____

Portions: _____

Preparation Process: _____

_____

_____

_____

_____

_____

_____

_____

_____

_____

_____

_____

_____

_____

_____

_____

_____

_____

_____

Recipe name: _____

Ingredients: _____

_____ _____

_____ _____

_____ _____

_____ _____

_____ _____

Cooking Time: _____

Portions: _____

Preparation Process: _____

_____

_____

_____

_____

_____

_____

_____

_____

_____

_____

_____

_____

_____

_____

_____

_____

_____

_____

Recipe name: _____

Ingredients: _____

_____   _____

_____   _____

_____   _____

_____   _____

_____   _____

Cooking Time: _____

Portions: _____

Preparation Process: _____

_____

_____

_____

_____

_____

_____

_____

_____

_____

_____

_____

_____

_____

_____

_____

_____

_____

_____

Recipe name: _____

Ingredients: _____

_____   _____

_____   _____

_____   _____

_____   _____

_____   _____

Cooking Time: _____

Portions: _____

Preparation Process: _____

_____

_____

_____

_____

_____

_____

_____

_____

_____

_____

_____

_____

_____

_____

_____

_____

_____

_____

_____

Recipe name: _____

Ingredients: _____

_____   _____

_____   _____

_____   _____

_____   _____

_____   _____

Cooking Time: _____

Portions: _____

Preparation Process: _____

_____

_____

_____

_____

_____

_____

_____

_____

_____

_____

_____

_____

_____

_____

_____

_____

_____

_____

Recipe name: _____

Ingredients: _____

_____ _____

_____ _____

_____ _____

_____ _____

_____

Cooking Time: _____

Portions: _____

Preparation Process: _____

_____

_____

_____

_____

_____

_____

_____

_____

_____

_____

_____

_____

_____

_____

_____

_____

_____

_____

Recipe name: _____

Ingredients: _____

_____ _____

_____ _____

_____ _____

_____ _____

_____ _____

Cooking Time: _____

Portions: _____

Preparation Process: _____

_____

_____

_____

_____

_____

_____

_____

_____

_____

_____

_____

_____

_____

_____

_____

_____

_____

_____

Recipe name: _____
Ingredients: _____

_____ _____

_____ _____

_____ _____

_____ _____

_____ _____

Cooking Time: _____
Portions: _____
Preparation Process: _____

_____

_____

_____

_____

_____

_____

_____

_____

_____

_____

_____

_____

_____

_____

_____

_____

_____

_____

_____

Recipe name: _____

Ingredients: _____

_____ _____

_____ _____

_____ _____

_____ _____

_____ _____

Cooking Time: _____

Portions: _____

Preparation Process: _____

_____

_____

_____

_____

_____

_____

_____

_____

_____

_____

_____

_____

_____

_____

_____

_____

_____

_____

_____

Recipe name: _____

Ingredients: _____

_____ _____

_____ _____

_____ _____

_____ _____

_____ _____

Cooking Time: _____

Portions: _____

Preparation Process: _____

_____

_____

_____

_____

_____

_____

_____

_____

_____

_____

_____

_____

_____

_____

_____

_____

_____

_____

_____

Recipe name: _____

Ingredients: _____

_____   _____

_____   _____

_____   _____

_____   _____

_____   _____

Cooking Time: _____

Portions: _____

Preparation Process: _____

_____

_____

_____

_____

_____

_____

_____

_____

_____

_____

_____

_____

_____

_____

_____

_____

_____

_____

_____

_____

_____

Recipe name: _____
Ingredients: _____

_____ _____
_____ _____
_____ _____
_____ _____
_____ _____

Cooking Time: _____
Portions: _____
Preparation Process:_____

_____
_____
_____
_____
_____
_____
_____
_____
_____
_____
_____
_____
_____
_____
_____
_____
_____
_____

Recipe name: _____
Ingredients: _____

_____   _____
_____   _____
_____   _____
_____   _____
_____   _____

Cooking Time: _____
Portions: _____
Preparation Process: _____

_____
_____
_____
_____
_____
_____
_____
_____
_____
_____
_____
_____
_____
_____
_____
_____
_____
_____
_____
_____

Recipe name: _____
Ingredients: _____

_____   _____

_____   _____

_____   _____

_____   _____

_____   _____

Cooking Time: _____
Portions: _____
Preparation Process: _____

_____

_____

_____

_____

_____

_____

_____

_____

_____

_____

_____

_____

_____

_____

_____

_____

_____

_____

_____

Recipe name: _____

Ingredients: _____

_____   _____

_____   _____

_____   _____

_____   _____

_____   _____

Cooking Time: _____

Portions: _____

Preparation Process: _____

_____

_____

_____

_____

_____

_____

_____

_____

_____

_____

_____

_____

_____

_____

_____

_____

_____

Recipe name: _____

Ingredients: _____

_____   _____

_____   _____

_____   _____

_____   _____

_____   _____

Cooking Time: _____

Portions: _____

Preparation Process:_____

_____

_____

_____

_____

_____

_____

_____

_____

_____

_____

_____

_____

_____

_____

_____

_____

_____

_____

Recipe name: _____

Ingredients: _____

_____ _____

_____ _____

_____ _____

_____ _____

_____ _____

Cooking Time: _____

Portions: _____

Preparation Process: _____

_____

_____

_____

_____

_____

_____

_____

_____

_____

_____

_____

_____

_____

_____

_____

_____

_____

_____

Recipe name: _____
Ingredients: _____

_____ _____

_____ _____

_____ _____

_____ _____

_____ _____

Cooking Time: _____
Portions: _____
Preparation Process: _____

_____

_____

_____

_____

_____

_____

_____

_____

_____

_____

_____

_____

_____

_____

_____

_____

_____

_____

Recipe name: _____

Ingredients: _____

_____ _____

_____ _____

_____ _____

_____ _____

_____ _____

Cooking Time: _____

Portions: _____

Preparation Process: _____

_____

_____

_____

_____

_____

_____

_____

_____

_____

_____

_____

_____

_____

_____

_____

_____

_____

_____

_____

_____

Recipe name: _____

Ingredients: _____

_____ _____

_____ _____

_____ _____

_____ _____

_____ _____

Cooking Time: _____

Portions: _____

Preparation Process: _____

_____

_____

_____

_____

_____

_____

_____

_____

_____

_____

_____

_____

_____

_____

_____

_____

_____

_____

_____

Recipe name: _____

Ingredients: _____

_____   _____

_____   _____

_____   _____

_____   _____

_____   _____

Cooking Time: _____

Portions: _____

Preparation Process:_____

_____

_____

_____

_____

_____

_____

_____

_____

_____

_____

_____

_____

_____

_____

_____

_____

_____

_____

_____

_____

_____

_____

Recipe name: _____
Ingredients: _____

_____   _____

_____   _____

_____   _____

_____   _____

_____   _____

Cooking Time: _____
Portions: _____
Preparation Process: _____

_____

_____

_____

_____

_____

_____

_____

_____

_____

_____

_____

_____

_____

_____

_____

_____

_____

_____

_____

Recipe name: _____

Ingredients: _____

_____   _____

_____   _____

_____   _____

_____   _____

_____   _____

Cooking Time: _____

Portions: _____

Preparation Process: _____

_____

_____

_____

_____

_____

_____

_____

_____

_____

_____

_____

_____

_____

_____

_____

_____

_____

_____

Recipe name: _____

Ingredients: _____

_____   _____

_____   _____

_____   _____

_____   _____

_____

Cooking Time: _____

Portions: _____

Preparation Process: _____

_____

_____

_____

_____

_____

_____

_____

_____

_____

_____

_____

_____

_____

_____

_____

_____

_____

Recipe name: _____

Ingredients: _____

_____ _____

_____ _____

_____ _____

_____ _____

_____ _____

Cooking Time: _____

Portions: _____

Preparation Process: _____

_____

_____

_____

_____

_____

_____

_____

_____

_____

_____

_____

_____

_____

_____

_____

_____

_____

_____

_____

_____

_____

_____

Recipe name: _____

Ingredients: _____

_____   _____

_____   _____

_____   _____

_____   _____

_____   _____

Cooking Time: _____

Portions: _____

Preparation Process: _____

_____

_____

_____

_____

_____

_____

_____

_____

_____

_____

_____

_____

_____

_____

_____

_____

_____

_____

Recipe name: _____

Ingredients: _____

_____ _____

_____ _____

_____ _____

_____ _____

_____ _____

Cooking Time: _____

Portions: _____

Preparation Process: _____

_____

_____

_____

_____

_____

_____

_____

_____

_____

_____

_____

_____

_____

_____

_____

_____

_____

Recipe name: _____

Ingredients: _____

_____ _____

_____ _____

_____ _____

_____ _____

_____ _____

Cooking Time: _____

Portions: _____

Preparation Process: _____

_____

_____

_____

_____

_____

_____

_____

_____

_____

_____

_____

_____

_____

_____

_____

_____

_____

_____

_____

_____

_____

Recipe name: _____
Ingredients: _____

_____ _____

_____ _____

_____ _____

_____ _____

_____ _____

Cooking Time: _____
Portions: _____
Preparation Process:_____

_____

_____

_____

_____

_____

_____

_____

_____

_____

_____

_____

_____

_____

_____

_____

_____

_____

_____

Recipe name: _____
Ingredients: _____

_____   _____
_____   _____
_____   _____
_____   _____
_____   _____

Cooking Time: _____
Portions: _____
Preparation Process: _____

_____
_____
_____
_____
_____
_____
_____
_____
_____
_____
_____
_____
_____
_____
_____
_____
_____

Recipe name: _____

Ingredients: _____

_____   _____

_____   _____

_____   _____

_____   _____

_____   _____

Cooking Time: _____

Portions: _____

Preparation Process: _____

_____

_____

_____

_____

_____

_____

_____

_____

_____

_____

_____

_____

_____

_____

_____

_____

_____

_____

Recipe name: _____

Ingredients: _____

_____ _____

_____ _____

_____ _____

_____ _____

_____ _____

Cooking Time: _____

Portions: _____

Preparation Process: _____

_____

_____

_____

_____

_____

_____

_____

_____

_____

_____

_____

_____

_____

_____

_____

_____

Recipe name: _____

Ingredients: _____

_____ _____

_____ _____

_____ _____

_____ _____

_____ _____

Cooking Time: _____

Portions: _____

Preparation Process: _____

_____

_____

_____

_____

_____

_____

_____

_____

_____

_____

_____

_____

_____

_____

_____

_____

_____

_____

_____

_____

_____

Recipe name: _____

Ingredients: _____

_____ _____

_____ _____

_____ _____

_____ _____

_____ _____

Cooking Time: _____

Portions: _____

Preparation Process: _____

_____

_____

_____

_____

_____

_____

_____

_____

_____

_____

_____

_____

_____

_____

_____

_____

_____

_____

_____

Recipe name: _____

Ingredients: _____

_____   _____

_____   _____

_____   _____

_____   _____

_____   _____

Cooking Time: _____

Portions: _____

Preparation Process: _____

_____

_____

_____

_____

_____

_____

_____

_____

_____

_____

_____

_____

_____

_____

_____

_____

_____

_____

_____

Recipe name: _____

Ingredients: _____

_____ _____

_____ _____

_____ _____

_____ _____

_____ _____

Cooking Time: _____

Portions: _____

Preparation Process: _____

_____

_____

_____

_____

_____

_____

_____

_____

_____

_____

_____

_____

_____

_____

_____

_____

_____

_____

Recipe name: _____

Ingredients: _____

_____   _____

_____   _____

_____   _____

_____   _____

_____   _____

Cooking Time: _____

Portions: _____

Preparation Process: _____

_____

_____

_____

_____

_____

_____

_____

_____

_____

_____

_____

_____

_____

_____

_____

_____

_____

_____

_____

_____

Recipe name: _____
Ingredients: _____

_____   _____
_____   _____
_____   _____
_____   _____
_____   _____

Cooking Time: _____
Portions: _____
Preparation Process: _____

_____
_____
_____
_____
_____
_____
_____
_____
_____
_____
_____
_____
_____
_____
_____
_____
_____
_____
_____

Recipe name: _____

Ingredients: _____

_____   _____

_____   _____

_____   _____

_____   _____

_____   _____

Cooking Time: _____

Portions: _____

Preparation Process: _____

_____

_____

_____

_____

_____

_____

_____

_____

_____

_____

_____

_____

_____

_____

_____

_____

_____

_____

_____

Recipe name: _____
Ingredients: _____

_____ _____

_____ _____

_____ _____

_____ _____

_____ _____

Cooking Time: _____
Portions: _____
Preparation Process:_____

_____

_____

_____

_____

_____

_____

_____

_____

_____

_____

_____

_____

_____

_____

_____

_____

_____

_____

_____

Recipe name: _____
Ingredients: _____

_____   _____
_____   _____
_____   _____
_____   _____
_____   _____

Cooking Time: _____
Portions: _____
Preparation Process: _____

_____
_____
_____
_____
_____
_____
_____
_____
_____
_____
_____
_____
_____
_____
_____
_____
_____
_____
_____

Recipe name: _____
Ingredients: _____

_____ _____

_____ _____

_____ _____

_____ _____

_____ _____

Cooking Time: _____
Portions: _____
Preparation Process: _____

_____

_____

_____

_____

_____

_____

_____

_____

_____

_____

_____

_____

_____

_____

_____

_____

_____

_____

_____

Recipe name: _____

Ingredients: _____

_____ _____

_____ _____

_____ _____

_____ _____

_____ _____

Cooking Time: _____

Portions: _____

Preparation Process: _____

_____

_____

_____

_____

_____

_____

_____

_____

_____

_____

_____

_____

_____

_____

_____

_____

_____

_____

_____

_____

Recipe name: _____
Ingredients: _____

_____   _____
_____   _____
_____   _____
_____   _____
_____   _____

Cooking Time: _____
Portions: _____
Preparation Process: _____

_____
_____
_____
_____
_____
_____
_____
_____
_____
_____
_____
_____
_____
_____
_____
_____
_____
_____
_____

Recipe name: _____

Ingredients: _____

_____   _____

_____   _____

_____   _____

_____   _____

_____   _____

Cooking Time: _____

Portions: _____

Preparation Process: _____

_____

_____

_____

_____

_____

_____

_____

_____

_____

_____

_____

_____

_____

_____

_____

_____

_____

_____

Recipe name: _____
Ingredients: _____

_____   _____
_____   _____
_____   _____
_____   _____
_____   _____

Cooking Time: _____
Portions: _____
Preparation Process:_____

_____
_____
_____
_____
_____
_____
_____
_____
_____
_____
_____
_____
_____
_____
_____
_____
_____
_____
_____
_____

www.ingramcontent.com/pod-product-compliance
Lightning Source LLC
Chambersburg PA
CBHW072101280526
45788CB00006B/2358